You Can Change Your Life By Law Of Implementation

Knowledge is power — implementation is transformation

VARSHA GHAGRE

Copyright © <2025> <Varsha Ghagre>

"This book will inspire you to move forward in life and guide you on the right path. It will be your companion in achieving success in every aspect of life."

Contents

Foreword... vi

Acknowledgments...viii

A Note to the Reader.. ix
Introduction.. x

1. Are you ready for good change.................................... 1

2. The law of Implementation....................................... 10

3. Obstacles to Implementation....................................29

4. First Step towards Implementation.............................55

5. Time, Timing and Timeliness...................................70

6. Not perfect just consistent..................................... 90

7. Change is choice made by real actions........................ 111

8. Power of NO and YES in Implementation...................... 120

9. Case Study and Success Stories................................ 138

10. Tools to Implementation.......................................148

Conclusion... 167

Foreword

Books are our real friends and teachers.
From childhood, we all read books — sometimes out of interest, sometimes because we had to — textbooks, biographies, or storybooks. As we grow, we start choosing books based on what we need and feel.

But this book is different.
In this book, Varsha shares one simple but powerful truth:
"You don't need to learn a hundred things. Just learn one thing and implement it — that alone can change your life."

And that's what makes this book so special.
Varsha has not written this book from theory. She has poured in her real-life experiences — her struggles, her growth, her transformation. And most importantly, she's kept it simple, small, and practical. With exercises, tools, and affirmations, this book is like a daily guide for anyone who wants real change.

I've known Miss Varsha for many years now.
I've seen her walk through pain, challenges, and difficult situations — and yet, she always smiles, always uplifts others, always shows up with love and courage. What she's doing through this book is not just writing — it's a service, an act of compassion.

She reminds me of a mother. A mother who says — *"If I've gone through pain, I want to make sure my children don't have to."*

And that's what she's doing. Through this book, she's offering a gift — a guide — to protect readers from failure, guilt, and regret. She's giving her best, straight from the heart.

This book especially speaks to young readers — those in the middle of building their future, finding their path, and facing life's pressures. And even though Varsha may not be a professional author, she has something most don't: **she practices what she teaches.**
That's her power. That's her authenticity.

So I say this to you — the reader:
Don't just read this book. *Apply it.* Choose even one thing from it and bring it into your daily life. Let this book be your guide, your friend, your gentle nudge forward.

Varsha, I wish you all the best for your beautiful journey — thank you for walking the path and lighting the way for others.

Dr Kishor Narad

M.D.(Homeopathy Clinic)

Nagpur

Acknowledgments

From the deepest corner of my heart,
I want to say a big, heartfelt **thank you** to everyone who became a part of this beautiful journey.

First, my deepest gratitude to **my mentor**, who believed in me, inspired me to write, and helped me see the strength I had within myself.

Without their guidance, this book may have remained just a dream.

I am also deeply thankful to **all my students** —
the ones I came to teach, but who, in truth, taught me.
They made me realize that I am a capable teacher,
that I have the power to support others in transforming their lives.
Their faith in me helped me believe in myself.

To **all my readers and listeners**,

thank you for trusting my words,
for giving your time and your heart to this journey.
Even if we have never met, your energy and presence have touched me deeply.

I know now that every small and big experience,
every happy and painful moment,
every relationship —
has shaped me and brought me to this place.
Each moment has taught me something valuable, and for all of it, I am truly grateful.

Whether it brought tears or smiles,
Every experience added color and life to the words of this book.
Everything — the good and the difficult — became a part of this creation.

Your love, your support, and your blessings were with me at every step —
 and that is why today, this dream has become real.

Maybe words will never be enough to express the depth of my gratitude,
 but from my soul to yours,
 please receive my heartfelt **Thank You**.

This journey was ours, is ours, and will always be ours.

With all my love and gratitude,
 – **Varsha**

A Note to the Reader

"Dear readers,

"I know that in today's world, everyone has access to knowledge. Everything is easily available and known. But just knowing something doesn't change your life — real transformation comes when you start living that knowledge and applying it in your daily life.

This book is my effort to show you how to do exactly that."

Everything I study and experience, I have written in this book to share with you. Just as I create content for my clients in my private coaching sessions, I have crafted something special here for you as well—something that will truly help you bring positive transformation in your life.
I encourage you to read this book once with focus, and then read it again with practice. You will surely see amazing results in your life."

Varsha Ghagre

May 2025

INTRODUCTION

Welcome, Dear friend!

I am Varsha.

For many years, I loved learning — reading books, attending seminars, and listening to inspiring talks.
But one day, I realized something very important:
Knowing is not enough.
Only doing things brings real change.

I noticed that many people, including myself, knew what was right — like eating healthy, studying regularly, staying positive — but very few actually *implemented* it.
That's when I discovered the **real missing link** in personal growth:
The Law of Implementation.

You can read hundreds of books, attend the best workshops, listen to the greatest teachers, but unless you take **real action**, nothing truly shifts.
Change doesn't happen just by learning —

Change happens when knowledge becomes action.

This book was born from my own journey.

When I first applied small daily actions — like changing my eating habits, sticking to a routine, saying "NO" to distractions, saying "YES" to my dreams — my life began to transform beautifully.

I lost weight naturally without gyms or medicine.
I built new habits that supported my dreams.
I developed inner strength and clarity.
I finally started living the life I once only imagined.

I realized that **implementation** is not hard — it simply needs understanding, support, and small, steady steps.

And now, I want to share this beautiful, powerful process with you.

This book is my hand extended to you, like a close friend, guiding you with love, hope, and practical steps.

I will walk beside you, helping you move from just *thinking* to *doing*, from *wishing* to *living*.

Inside this book, you will find:

- Clear steps for implementing changes

- Real-life examples you can relate to

- Affirmations time to keep you strong

- Simple implementation time to keep you moving forward

- Worksheets to track your progress

I have written every page with the pure intention that you, too, will experience the magic I experienced — The magic that comes when dreams meet action.

> Are you ready to start your beautiful journey of real transformation?
> Are you ready to live the life you dream about?

If yes, then hold my hand — and let's walk this path together.

With love and faith,
 Varsha :)

❖   Now Affirmations Time :

>>   Take a deep breath, feel the energy within you, and read the affirmations out loud with belief <<

"I turn knowledge into action and action into success."

"I am committed to implementing positive changes in my life."

"I learn, I apply, and I grow stronger every day."

"I honor my journey by taking small, powerful steps forward."

"I believe that real change comes through real action."

"I am proud of every step I take toward my dreams."

"I am living proof that small actions create big transformations."

"I inspire others by being true to my path."

"Through my journey, I open doors for others to believe in themselves."

"My story is a light for others to start their journey."

1. Are you ready for Good Change

Today, everyone knows what's good for them — but how many people actually apply that goodness in their lives?

Probably not many. Because just knowing something doesn't create change.

To create real change, we must take action.

And that action only begins when we ask ourselves one powerful question:

"Am I ready for this positive change?"

Only when the answer is "Yes," does true transformation begin.

But most people never really reach that "Yes."

Let me share an example from my own experience.

One of my students, Kavita, was studying in the first year of engineering.

She failed her exams due to some personal struggles, and for almost a year, she couldn't clear her subjects.

Then, during her second attempt, she still couldn't pass.
Her family lost patience and told her clearly,
"If you can't handle this, quit engineering. We'll arrange your marriage instead."

That moment shook her deeply — because Kavita had a dream — she wanted to be independent, stand on her own feet, and marry someone she truly loved.
If her studies had ended, that dream would have died.

That's when she came to me and said,
"Ma'am, please guide me. I want to pass my exams no matter what."

I asked her just one thing: "Why do you want this so deeply?"

She replied with full clarity —

"Because I want to build my own life. I want to be strong. I want to choose my future, not let others choose it for me."

Once her reason was strong, the change came naturally.

That very year, she cleared her backlog, and over the next three years, she passed with excellent marks and completed her degree successfully.

See, some people study just to pass exams.

But Kavita studied to stand on her own feet — to take charge of her life.

That's when true change happened.

Change is not some distant thing that happens only to "lucky" people.

Change is not something you have to chase far away.

Change begins the very moment you say, "Yes, I am ready."

This book you are holding is not just a collection of words.

It's an invitation — an open door to a better, brighter life that is waiting for you.

Inside you, there are dreams that are still alive, still hopeful.

You don't have to create them — they already exist within you.

Now, it's time to give them wings through action... through implementation.

Are you ready to believe in your own power?

Are you ready to take small, gentle steps toward big, beautiful changes?

If your heart whispers even a soft "yes," then you are already halfway there.
You don't need to know every step.
You don't need to be perfect.
You just need a little willingness —

A small spark of hope inside that says,
"Maybe I can."

Most people wait for the "perfect time" to start.
They think, "I'll begin when I have more time, more money, more confidence."
But the truth is simple:
The perfect time is always now.
Waiting keeps you stuck.
Starting sets you free.

Good change doesn't mean turning your whole life upside down in one day.
It doesn't mean working harder, pushing harder, or stressing more.
Good change is about one small step today,
another small step tomorrow,
and a gentle journey that builds real miracles over time.

One day, you will look back and realize,
"Wow, I really changed my life... just by starting."

In this journey, you will not walk alone.
I will be with you through these pages — cheering for you, guiding you, and celebrating every small victory.
Because small victories are how big dreams come true.

> You are stronger than you think.
> You are more capable than you believe.
> Everything you hope for is already much closer than it seems.

So once again, I ask you softly, lovingly, and with full faith:
Are you ready for good change?

If your heart says even the tiniest "yes,"

Then welcome, my dear friend —
Your most beautiful journey is beginning today.

➤ Now implementations Time

Take a deep breath. Close your eyes for a moment.
 Now, answer these simple questions in your heart or write down here:

1. Am I willing to believe that change is possible for me?

____

____

2. Am I open to taking small steps every day?

____

____

3. Am I ready to trust the process, even if I don't see instant results?

4. Will I be kind and patient with myself as I grow?

If you answered **"Yes"** to even one of these questions —
Congratulations! > You have already started your journey toward a better life.

Now, place your hand on your heart and say softly:

"I am ready. I am open. I am moving toward a beautiful change."

Welcome to your new beginning!

NOTES: *(My learning from this chapter)*

2. The Law of Implementation

"Strategy without implementation is a daydream."

— *Japanese Proverb*

What is Implementation?

Implementation means turning your *knowing* into *doing*.
 It's the bridge between *dreaming* and *achieving*.

You can read hundreds of self-help books.
 You can attend all the workshops in the world.
 But unless you actually apply what you learn — nothing changes.

Implementation is when the idea in your mind becomes action in your life.
 It's when "I should" becomes "I did."
 It's not always big or fancy. Sometimes, it's as simple as drinking water when your body needs it, or saying "No" when your heart says no.

Let's go deeper with some simple stories.

Principles of Implementation

1. Clarity Leads to Action

When you know exactly what you want, you move faster and with more confidence.

If your goal is not clear, your actions will also be confused and slow.

"When the mind is clear, the path becomes visible."

Example:

I once asked one of my students what her goal was. She said, "I want to be successful."

I smiled and asked, "What does success look like for you?"

She paused. "Maybe... working for myself?"

We talked more, and she realized her actual dream was to run a small baking business from home.

Once she said it clearly, her whole body lit up.

Within two weeks, she had made a logo and taken her first two cake orders.

Lesson:
Vague goals confuse you. Clear goals activate you.

2. Decisions Begin the Journey

Nothing changes until you **make a decision** inside your heart.
  Saying "YES" to yourself is the real beginning of any journey.

"Your decision activates your destiny."

Example:

I remember when I decided to stop eating after 7 PM.
  There was no pressure, no outside rule — just a choice I made for myself.
  From that day, my body started feeling lighter.
  Friends would tempt me at parties: "Just one bite!"
  But my heart had already said yes to my health — so I gently said no to everything else.

Lesson:

Real journeys begin the moment you decide — not when you feel fully ready.

3. Timeliness is Power

Taking the **right action at the right time** makes all the difference.

If you delay too much, doubts will start growing in your mind.

> *"If you don't act on time, it's like having a seed but never planting it."*

Example:

One of my clients wanted to say sorry to her sister after a big fight.

She kept thinking, "I'll call tomorrow." But tomorrow kept slipping away.

By the time she gathered the courage, her sister had moved cities — and their bond was never the same.

One message could've saved a lot of pain.

Lesson:

Timely action can heal wounds and open doors. Waiting too long can close them.

4. Consistent Action is Better than Big Efforts Once

Small steps taken daily create bigger changes than huge efforts taken once in a while.

> *"Success is born in the repetition of action."*

Example:

My friend and I both wanted to lose weight.
Neha would go to the gym once a week and push herself hard — but then rest for many days.
I chose a different path: 20 minutes of walking every morning, no matter what.
In 3 months, I felt fitter and lighter.
she said, "How did you change so fast?"
I smiled: "Because I didn't stop."

Lesson:
Small daily steps are stronger than occasional giant leaps.

5. Inner Balance Brings Better Results

When your heart, mind, and soul all agree, you take action happily and powerfully.
Inner peace gives outer success.

"The most powerful implementation comes from inner harmony."

Example:

A woman in my workshop shared that she joined Zumba classes to get fit — but hated it.
She loved dancing but didn't like the pressure of a gym.
So, she switched to dancing freely at home to her favorite music.
Now, she moves joyfully every day — and her energy has doubled.

Lesson:
When your heart is in it, implementation flows like water.

6. Awareness Keeps You Focused

When you stay aware of what you are doing and why you are doing it, you make better decisions.

> *"Action without awareness is just activity."*

Example:

A man once told me he was busy all the time but felt unfulfilled.

He woke up, worked, scrolled on his phone, helped the family — but still felt something was missing.

When we talked deeper, he realized: he wasn't doing anything aligned with his deeper purpose.

He added just 10 minutes of sketching every night — something he loved as a child — and his days started feeling meaningful again.

Lesson:
Be busy, yes — but don't forget to be intentional.

Implementation in Different Areas

1. Career Goals

We all have career dreams — a better job, a new business, or doing work that we actually love. But let's be honest — daydreaming about a corner office won't get us the keys!

I remember a friend's daughter who always said, "I want to become a graphic designer." She had talent, for sure! But months went by… no new skills, no online course, not even a simple resume update.

One day I asked, "So, what did you do today for your dream?" She replied, "I searched for cool Instagram designers for inspiration."

Inspiration is great, but let's face it — Instagram scrolling is not an implementation!

> **Steps You Can Take:**

- Update your resume (yes, even if it feels boring).

- Apply to 2 jobs a week — start somewhere.

- Watch a 20-minute tutorial and *actually* practice.

- Write down your business idea and take one action — like buying a domain or talking to a mentor.

"Dreams don't work unless you do. Even one step counts!"

2. Relationships

Who doesn't want love, peace, and connection? But "I care about you" is not a one-time statement — it's a daily act.

My own lesson came during a silly argument with my sister. We both waited for the other to say sorry. Days passed. Finally, I messaged her a meme that said, "Still mad but also hungry." She laughed, we talked, and all was well.

Moral? Love lives in little things. Not grand speeches.

Steps You Can Take:

- Walk while talking on the phone.
- eat your food with gratitude, love and respect
- while eating no tv and screen only peaceful eating
- while eating try to chew your food maximum
- Eat one homemade meal instead of ordering out.

- Add one fruit to your daily diet.

- Sleep 15 minutes earlier each night.

***"Relationships don't grow on good intentions —
they grow on small, kind actions."***

3. Health and Wellness

We all know what we *should* do: eat better, move
more, sleep early.

But most of us live in "I'll start Monday" mode —
and Monday never comes!

One day, I told myself: "Today, I'll just go for a
10-minute walk. That's it." I ended up walking for
25 minutes while calling a friend. Bonus: I felt great
and didn't even realize I exercised!

Steps You Can Take:

- Walk while talking on the phone.

- Eat one homemade meal instead of ordering out.

- Add one fruit to your daily diet.

- Sleep 15 minutes earlier each night.

Health is not one big decision. It's a hundred tiny choices you make every day.

4. Money and Finance

We all say, "I need to save more." But when the sale signs say *'Buy 1, Get Regret Free,'* we forget everything!

One of my friends started tracking her expenses in a simple notebook — not an app, just pen and paper. In the first month, she discovered she spent ₹1,200 just on "extra chai and snacks."

Now she makes chai at home and saves that ₹1,200 every month — which she calls her "spa fund!"

Steps You Can Take:

- Write down every rupee you spend for one week.

- Set a small saving target: ₹50/day = ₹1,500/month.

- Avoid impulse buys — ask: "Do I really need this, or am I just bored?"

Saving money isn't about big sacrifices. It's about small, mindful choices.

5. Personal Growth:

How many of us say, "That book changed my life!" — and then don't apply even one idea from it?

Yes, I've done that too! I once read a book on morning routines… while lying in bed at 11:30 AM.

The truth is, learning is fun, but growing takes practice.

> Steps You Can Take:

- After reading or watching something inspiring, write down ONE thing you'll apply today.

- Start journaling 5 minutes every morning or night.

- Pick one habit to build each month — and track it on a sticky note!

Personal growth isn't about how much you know. It's about how much you apply.

"Implementation is not a big mountain to climb.
 It's a series of small, daily, loving actions toward your best life."

> Start where you are.
> Do what you can.
> Trust yourself.

Implementation is the secret that will turn your dreams into reality.

⊙ *Now implementation time*

Answer these 3 simple questions in notes below:

1. **What is one good thing you already know but have not started doing yet?** *(Example: Meditate 5 minutes daily.)*

2. **What is one tiny action you can take today?** *(Example: Download a meditation app.)*

3. **When will you start?** *(Example: Tonight before sleeping.)*

> *Write it.*
> *Decide it.*
> *Do it!*

You have just started your journey of real change!

NOTES: *(My learning from this chapter)*

25

⊙ Now Affirmations Time :

>> Take a deep breath, feel the energy within you, and read the affirmations out loud with belief <<

"I turn my thoughts into action with ease and joy."

"I implement my goals with clarity, courage, and commitment."

"I am the creator of my reality through what I do each day."

"Implementation is my superpower — I follow through, and I thrive."
"I take action with confidence and purpose."

"Every small step I take moves me closer to my goals."

"I do what needs to be done — now, not later."

"My actions today create the results I desire tomorrow."

3. Obstacles to Implementation

Life changes when we start **doing**.

But many times, even when we know the right thing, we don't act on it.

Why?

Because **small invisible obstacles** stop us quietly.

Let's gently look at these obstacles together — not to judge ourselves, but to understand, and lovingly move forward.

1. Short-Term Benefits

Short-term benefits are the tiny comforts or quick rewards we get **right now** when we avoid doing something difficult.
It feels good in the moment — but later, it brings regret.

Example:

As I had shared with you in the beginning, through the Law of Implementation, I transformed my unhealthy body into a healthy one. One of my first steps was to start eating before 7 PM. Then, I made another decision — I began cooking my meals in earthen pots instead of aluminum ones.

In the beginning, yes — it took a little extra time and effort. I wasn't used to it. But slowly, it became easier. It even started saving me time, because I was more mindful and present during cooking.

During this journey, many of my friends and relatives would say, "Oh, it must be taking so much time. And earthen pots use more gas, right?" I would smile and say, "Yes, maybe a little more gas… maybe ₹100 extra a month."

But I also noticed something important.

Many people know that cooking in an earthen pot is much healthier for the body.
 But just because it uses ₹100 more gas in a month, they avoid it.
 They continue cooking in aluminum or non-stick utensils, not realizing that one day, this choice may cost them ₹1,000 in doctor's fees, in medicines, in pain, and in regret and even more in health issues.

For saving just ₹100 today, they risk their entire health tomorrow.

Don't let small comforts today steal your big health, happiness, and dreams of tomorrow.

Sometimes, doing the right thing may take a little more effort in the beginning — but the rewards are far greater in the long run.

2. Following Family, Friends, and Society Blindly

When we are children, we're taught so many good things at school:

- Don't waste water.

- Throw garbage only in the dustbin.

- Don't eat while watching TV.

- Always speak politely.

But when we come home, the story is often very different.

We see…

- Parents watching TV while eating dinner.

- The tap running for long while brushing or washing hands.

- People throwing empty wrappers out of car windows.

- Adults shouting at each other or using harsh words in front of kids.

My own Life Example :

I once visited a relative's home. Their little child refused to eat until the TV was turned on. When I asked him, "Don't you learn in school not to watch TV while eating?"
He said, "Yes, but mama and papa also do that every day!"

That hit me hard.
We keep teaching children what's *right*, but we forget that they learn more by watching us than by listening to us.

And slowly, they start believing:

"Knowing is enough — doing is not important."

More Examples:

1. Wasting Water:

    A child learns in school that water is precious.
    But at home, he sees buckets overflowing, people letting the tap run while washing clothes or vehicles.

    He thinks: *"Why should I save water when no one else does?"*

2. Littering:

    You visit a tourist spot. There are dustbins everywhere, yet people throw chips packets and bottles on the ground.

    A child sees this and believes:
    "Maybe the rule is just for the classroom, not for real life."

3. Healthy Eating Habits:

You want to eat healthy, but at family gatherings everyone is eating junk and saying:

"One day won't harm you!"
But slowly, *one day* becomes *every day*.

♡ **Heart-Touching Truth:**

When we follow the crowd blindly — even if it's family, friends, or society — we lose our own values.
We stop doing what we know is right, just to fit in or avoid judgment.

But real change doesn't come from blending in.
It comes from standing out — with love, patience, and quiet strength.

3. Expecting Others to Change First

Today, it's easy to access knowledge. We all know what's right and wrong — we've been taught since childhood.
But still, most of us expect *others* to change first.
We say things like,
"Why should I adjust? Let them do the right thing first."

We believe that the change should begin from the outside — from family, society, or even strangers.

Remember how I mentioned earlier — kids are taught in school:
"Speak the truth."
"Don't eat while watching TV."
But what happens at home?

Often, parents themselves break those same rules.
 They watch TV while eating, and they don't even realize a little child is watching and learning.
 And slowly, the child adopts the same habits.
 That's what happened to me too.

Before I began practicing the Law of Implementation, I also had that child within me — the one who knew what was right, but waited for others to change first.

Let me share a real incident.
 Once, my friend's family and mine were traveling together. Her husband had great knowledge — about health, medicine, politics, and more. He was well-read and spoke confidently.

But during the trip, I noticed something.

He took medicine just out of tiredness, without even trying to rest or hydrate first.

Later, we visited an aunt's house who was on multiple medications.

When she shared her concerns, this same man told her not to take too many medicines — but I noticed he himself had already taken a tablet for a small reason, like tiredness from travel.

I was surprised.

On one hand, he spoke about health and natural wellness.

On the other, his actions were just the opposite.

This is what I realized:

Many people have knowledge.

They even teach others.

But they don't implement it themselves.

And they often expect *others* to be the ones who change first.

But how long will this continue?

Change doesn't start with others.

It starts within us.

As long as we keep holding on to old beliefs and

excuses — that inner child will keep expecting someone else to take the first step.

But when you choose to implement what you know…
You become the example.
You become the change.

4. Procrastination (Delaying Actions)

Let's be honest — we've all done it.

We say,

"I'll start tomorrow."
"I'll do it after this one thing."
"I need to be in the right mood first."

But the truth is… that "tomorrow" often never comes. And without realizing it, we keep pushing our important goals further and further away.

Let me give you a real example.

One of my students once told me, "Ma'am, I really want to top the exam this time."
He had the ability — no doubt. But every day, he'd come home from collage, and instead of studying, he'd get distracted — a little online gaming, some

chatting, a bit of scrolling.
   she kept saying, "I'll study seriously from tomorrow."
 And guess what? Tomorrow kept slipping away.
 When the results came, he looked at me and said with a heavy heart,

"Ma'am, I wish I had started when I said I would."

The regret was real.

To be honest, I've done this too.
 There were days I planned to write a chapter for this very book — but then, I'd start scrolling on my phone, or suddenly remember to organize my cupboard or reply to a random message.
 It felt like I was being "busy"… but not with the right thing.

>> These tiny delays?

They don't seem like much.
But slowly, they pile up — and one day, you find yourself stuck, wishing you had just started earlier.

  Here's what I've learned: You don't have to do everything.
 You don't need the perfect day, perfect mood, or perfect plan.

Just take one honest step today.
Even if it's small. Even if it's not perfect.

* Write one paragraph.
* Read two pages.
* Do 5 minutes of walking.

That one step creates momentum — and once you begin, it gets easier to keep going.

"The journey doesn't start with motivation. It starts with action."

4. Fear

- Fear doesn't always scream.
  Sometimes, it whispers quietly inside your heart…

  "What if I fail?"
  "What if people laugh at me?"
  "What if I'm not good enough?"

- It can make your chest feel heavy. Your feet freeze. Your dreams stay locked inside.

Example:

I remember one woman in my class. She was full of creativity — amazing ideas, deep thoughts.
 One day, I asked her, "Why don't you start your own blog or business?"

 She smiled, paused, and said,
 "I think I'm not ready yet... What if I post something and people don't like it? What if I mess up?"

And just like that — her dream got delayed again.

Honestly, I've felt it too.
 When I started writing this book, I had fears in my mind:
 "Will people even read this?"
 "What if someone criticizes my writing?"
 But then I reminded myself:
 "This book is not about being perfect. It's about being real."
 And I took one step… and then another.

So how do we face fear?

It starts by being honest.
Say it out loud:

"I feel scared of __."
Naming the fear takes away half its power.

Then — take just one small, brave step.
 Not a big leap. Not a perfect move.
 Just one tiny action in the direction of your dream.

>> *Here's the magic:*

 The moment you take that step, fear begins to shrink.
 It no longer controls you.
 You start to feel stronger, bolder, freer.

Remember:

Your dreams are bigger than your doubts.
And you are always stronger than your fear.

5. Lack of Clarity

Sometimes, it's not about being lazy or avoiding the goal — it's about feeling **confused**. You want to change, but you don't know exactly where to start, so you stay stuck.

Example:

Me and my friend both decided to lose weight. We had the same goal, but there was one difference — while I took small, clear steps, she was overwhelmed by confusion.

She'd say things like:

"Should I join a gym?"
"Should I follow a strict diet?"
"Should I do yoga or run?"

All these options confused her, and before she knew it, she hadn't taken any action at all.

I, on the other hand, decided to focus on one simple thing at a time. One day, I chose to have **dinner before 7 PM**, and the next month, I made a small commitment to **chew my food properly**. Both felt like small steps, but they made a difference. They gave me clarity.

This is how you break free from confusion.

I've been there too — overwhelmed with options. But I learned that if you don't know what to do, don't try to figure out everything at once. Just pick **one small, clear action** you can take today.

Here's what I did:

- I started with a **10-minute walk**.

- I decided to **drink 2 extra glasses of water**.

- I chose to **chew my food properly** instead of rushing through meals

---

Message from My Heart:

Obstacles are not your enemies.
They are just small clouds passing by.
The sun of your strength is always shining behind them.

>> Awareness is your key.
>> Small actions are your bridge.
>> Believing in yourself is your superpower.

Together, let's gently move through these obstacles
—

And step into the life you truly deserve.

⊙ *Now implementation time*

Clear Your Obstacles to Implementation

Write your answers honestly Here:

1. Short-Term Benefits Trap

- **Question:**

  What short-term comfort is stopping me from taking the right action?
  (Example: Watching TV instead of exercising.)

2. Following Family, Friends, Society

- **Question:**

  Where am I following others blindly, even when I know what's right for me?

  (Example: Eating junk food at parties because everyone else is.)

3. Procrastination

- **Question:**

  What important thing am I delaying again and again?

  (Example: Starting my morning walk.)

4. Fear

- **Question:**
  What am I afraid will happen if I take action?

  (Example: Fear of failing in a new business.)

5. Lack of Clarity

- **Question:**
  What is still unclear to me about my next step?
  (Example: I want to eat healthy, but I don't know what foods to choose.)

Step 1: Identify Your Biggest Obstacle

Take a deep breath.
 Ask yourself gently:

>>   What is one obstacle that is stopping me from taking action today?

Short-term comfort
 Following family/friends/society blindly
 Procrastination (delaying)
 Fear
 Lack of clarity
Something else: _____________

Write it here:

____

____

____

____

Step 2: Talk to Your Obstacle with Love

Imagine your obstacle is a small child inside you — not something to fight, but something to **understand**.

Complete this sentence:

"Dear ______ (obstacle name), I understand you are trying to protect me, but I lovingly choose to grow beyond you."

> Example: "Dear procrastination, I understand you are trying to protect me from hard work, but I lovingly choose to move forward."

Write your line here:

Step 3: Choose One Tiny Step

Now ask yourself:

\>\> What is **one small step** I can take today to move forward?

(Example: Walk for 5 minutes, study one topic, make one healthy meal.)

Write it here:

Step 4: Affirm Your Power

Repeat this to yourself softly:

"I am bigger than my obstacles. I choose action. I choose growth. I choose me."
(Write the Affirmation here)

Bonus Tip:

Put today's small step as a **tiny reminder on your phone** or **stick a note** where you can see it.
 Let your dreams stay in front of your eyes and close to your heart.

NOTES: *(My learning from this chapter)*

⊙ Now Affirmations Time :

\>\>   Take a deep breath, feel the energy within you, and read the affirmations out loud with belief   \<\<

- *"Action feels good, and I enjoy getting things done."*

- *"I am in control of my time and energy."*

- *"I begin now. The perfect moment is this one."*

- *"I take small steps, and they create big change."*
"My mind is calm, my vision is clear."

- *"I give myself permission to take one step at a time."*

- *"Clarity comes through action, and I trust the process."*

- *"The more I move, the clearer my path becomes."*

- *"I listen to my inner guidance. It always leads me right."*

- *"I am focused, intentional, and aligned with my purpose."*

- *"I have everything I need within me to succeed."*

- *"I am braver than I feel, stronger than I think."*

- *"Each time I act despite fear, I grow more powerful."*

- *"Fear is a signal, not a stop sign. I move forward anyway."*

- *"My dreams are bigger than my doubts."*

4. First Steps Toward Implementation

1. You must know what you want.

Why it matters:

Clarity is the starting point for all action. If your goal is unclear, your actions will be scattered and ineffective.

What it means:

You need to clearly define what you want. It could be a healthier body, a peaceful mind, a successful business, or better relationships.

How to do it:

- Ask yourself: *"What do I truly want right now?"*

- Write it down in one clear sentence.

- Be specific. For example: "I want to exercise 10 minutes every day" is better than "I want to be fit."

2. You must truly desire it.

Why it matters:

Without genuine desire, you won't have the motivation to follow through when things get tough. True desire gives you emotional energy to act.

What it means:

Your goal must matter to you—not just because others say it's important, but because *you* feel connected to it deeply.

How to do it:

- Ask: *"Why do I want this?"*

- Feel the emotion behind the goal: excitement, freedom, love, confidence.

- Visualize your success and let it light a fire in you.

3. You must know how you will get it.

Why it matters:

Desire alone isn't enough—you need a path. A clear method or plan gives you direction and makes your goal feel possible.

What it means:

You don't need to know *every* step, but you do need to know where to begin and what tools or support you'll need.

How to do it:

- Break the goal into small steps.

- Ask: *"What is one action I can take today?"*

- Find resources: books, mentors, videos, or courses.

- Create a basic plan, even if it's just a starting point.

4. You must be ready to take action.

Why it matters:

No amount of dreaming, planning, or wishing will bring results unless you take real action. Action is the bridge between your inner vision and outer reality.

What it means:

Being *ready* doesn't mean you're fearless or perfect—it means you're willing to move forward *despite* doubts or discomfort. You're prepared to step into the process and make progress, one step at a time.

How to do it:

- **Start small:** Take one tiny step today, no matter how simple.

- **Let go of perfection:** Progress matters more than perfection.

- **Use momentum:** Once you act, the next step becomes easier.

- **Remind yourself:** *"I don't have to be great to start, but I have to start to be great."*

⊙ *Now implementation time*

Goal: To guide you through the initial steps of clarifying, desiring, planning, and acting on your goals.

Part 1: Clarify Your Goal (What Do You Really Want?)

1. **Write down one goal** that is important to you. It can be related to health, career, relationships, or personal growth.

2. **Be specific**: Write it in a clear and focused sentence. Avoid vague statements like "I want to be fit." Instead, say something like, "I want to walk 30 minutes every day."

   Example: "I want to complete a 5k run in 3 months."

Part 2: Identify Your Desire (Why Do You Want This?)

1. **Dig deep and find the reason behind your goal.**

   Ask yourself:

   - Why is this goal important to me?

   - How will it make me feel when I achieve it?

   - What difference will it make in my life?

2. **Describe your emotional connection** to the goal. This should stir excitement, love, or passion for your vision.

   Example: "I want to run the 5k because it will help me feel healthier, more energetic, and confident. It will show me that I can achieve something I once thought was hard."

Part 3: Break it Down (How Will You Get There?)

1. **Identify the first small step** you need to take today to move toward your goal. This is your starting point, no matter how small it may seem.

2. **Write down the resources** you need to get started: books, tools, courses, or a mentor.

3. **Create a simple plan**:

   - What can you do today to make progress?

   - What's the next small action for tomorrow?

4. **Example:**
   Today's action: "Buy running shoes."

   Tomorrow's action: "Start with a 10-minute walk."

Part 4: Ready to Act (Take Action!)

1. **Commit to the first small action today.** It doesn't have to be perfect, just the next logical step.

2. **Set a reminder** for yourself to take the first action:

   o Write it on a sticky note.

   o Set a phone alarm with the reminder.

3. **Reflect on your progress**: After completing your first action, write down how it felt. Did you feel good? Did it seem less scary than you thought?

   Example: "I felt excited to buy the shoes, and it made the goal feel more real."

____

____

Part 5: Accountability Check

1. **Find an accountability partner**: It can be a friend, family member, or colleague who will check in with you about your progress.

2. **Create a weekly check-in** for your goal. You can use a journal, tracker, or app to review:

    o   What have you done this week?

    o   What challenges did you face?

    o   How can you improve for next week?

____

____

Reflection:

- What part of this process feels most challenging for you?

- What part excites you the most?

- How can you make this process more fun for yourself?

NOTES: *(My learning from this chapter)*

⊙ Now Affirmations Time :

\>\>   Take a deep breath, feel the energy within you, and read the affirmations out loud with belief \<\<

- *I am clear about what I truly want.*

- *My goals are aligned with my inner truth.*

- *I Truly Want This*
- *Clarity flows to me with ease and confidence.*

- *I deeply desire this change, and I welcome it into my life.*

- *My heart is fully committed to my goal.*

- *My desire is strong, focused, and unshakable.*

- *My desire is strong, focused, and unshakable.*

- *The path ahead is becoming clearer with each step I take.*

- *I trust the process and take one step at a time.*

- *I am guided by wisdom, insight, and purpose.*

- *I Know How to Get It*

- *The path ahead is becoming clearer with each step I take.*

- *I trust the process and take one step at a time.*

- *I am guided by wisdom, insight, and purpose.*

- *I Am Ready to Take Action*

- *I am ready now. I take action with confidence.*

- *Even the smallest step moves me forward.*

- *I turn intention into action every single day.*

5. Time, Timing & Timeliness

1. Time

What is it? Time is just… there. Seconds, minutes, hours—it flows, whether you like it or not. It's neutral.

Like this: Imagine looking at your phone. It's 9:00 AM. That's time. It doesn't care what you're doing. It just moves.

Why it matters: Since you can't pause or rewind time, the best thing to do is use it well—because once it's gone, it's gone.

2. Timing

What is it? Timing is *when* you choose to do something.

Like this: You've got a 10 AM flight. You leave your house at 8 AM. Perfect timing!

Why it matters: You might have the best plan in the world, but if you do it at the wrong time, it might flop. Timing is the secret sauce to making actions work.

3. Timeliness

What is it? Timeliness is being on the dot—not too early, not too late.

Like this: You reached the airport on time and got your seat. That's timeliness.

Why it matters: It shows discipline and awareness. It also keeps you moving forward without stress.

Sum up of above

- **Time** is the ticking clock.

- **Timing** is when you *decide* to act.

- **Timeliness** is *doing it at the right moment.*

1. Why action within the right time matters

Why Taking Action at the Right Time Matters

Think of it like catching a flight:

- **You decided** you want to go to Mumbai. (Clarity)

- **You really want** to be there. (Desire)

- **You booked the flight.** (Direction)
  But...

If you **don't reach the airport on time,**

You'll **miss the flight,**

Even though you knew what to do and had the ticket.

Right action at the right time = success.
Delay = missed opportunity.

Example 1: *Submitting a Job Application*

- My Goal: Apply for a new job.

- Why Is Timing Important?:
  The company closes applications in 3 days.

- What Time Will I Take Action?:
  Today evening at 7 PM, I will update my resume and send the application.

- What Will Happen If I Delay?:
  I may miss the deadline and lose a great opportunity.

- **Affirmation:**

  "I act at the right time and grab the right opportunities."

Example 2: *Starting Healthy Eating*

- My Goal: Start eating healthier meals.

- Why Is Timing Important?:
  If I don't plan my meals early, I may grab junk food when I'm hungry.

- What Time Will I Take Action?:
  Every night at 9 PM, I will plan my next day's meals.

- What Will Happen If I Delay?:
  I will continue unhealthy habits and feel low energy.

- **Affirmation:**
  "I prepare ahead and honor my health with timely actions."

Example 3: *Studying for an Exam*

- My Goal: Study 2 chapters every day for my upcoming exam.

- Why Is Timing Important?:
  If I start late, I will feel stressed and unprepared.

- What Time Will I Take Action?:
  Every afternoon from 4 PM to 6 PM.

- What Will Happen If I Delay?:
  I might have to rush last-minute and score poorly.

- **Affirmation:**
  "I study on time and prepare calmly for my success."

⊙ *Now implementation time*

Strengthen Your Timing Muscle

Step 1: Pick ONE goal you want to achieve this month.

(Example: Start walking daily, finish a project, study for an exam.)

Step 2: Answer these questions:

1. **What is my goal?**
   → (Write clearly.)

2. **Why does timing matter for this goal?**
   → (Explain why starting on time is important.)

3. **When exactly will I take action?**
   → (Choose specific days and times.)

4. **What can go wrong if I delay?**
   → (Write the risk of waiting too long.)

5. **My Power Affirmation:**

→ (Write one sentence to motivate yourself.)

1. **Goal:** Start 10 minutes of yoga daily.

2. **Why Timing Matters:** If I don't fix a time, I'll keep delaying.

3. **Action Time:** Every morning at 7 AM after brushing my teeth.

4. **Risk If I Delay:** I may feel lazy and miss my health goals.

5. **Power Affirmation:**

→ "I honor my body and take care of it on time."

Here's a modified version of the **Time, Timing & Timeliness** exercises with real-life examples to make them more relatable:

Exercise 1: Time Inventory

Goal: To help you assess how you spend your time and identify areas for improvement.

Instructions:

1. **Track your time**: For the next 3 days, keep a simple log of how you spend your time. Divide your day into hourly blocks, and record what you do during each block (e.g., work, exercise, social media, meals, etc.).

2. **Identify patterns**: After 3 days, review your log.

   o **Real-life example**: Imagine you track your time for 3 days and realize you're spending 2 hours each day on social media, but you didn't find time to work on a personal project you've been meaning to start.

   o Notice if you spend too much time on distractions (social media, TV, etc.) or procrastinate on key activities (work, study, etc.).

3. **Action**: Based on your time inventory, make a plan to adjust your day. Prioritize tasks that help you achieve your goals and reduce time spent on distractions.

   Example: If you're spending too much time on social media, you might decide to limit social media usage to 30 minutes a day and replace it with something more productive, like learning a new skill or working on a goal.

The 5-Minute Rule

Goal: To help you start action immediately, no matter how big or small the task is.

Instructions:

1. **Pick a task you've been putting off**: This could be something big, like starting a business, or something small, like responding to emails or cleaning your house.

   o   **example**: You've been wanting to clean your kitchen for days, but keep putting it off. Instead of dreading the task, set a timer for 5 minutes.

2. **Set a timer for 5 minutes**: Commit to working on the task for just 5 minutes. Often, starting is the hardest part, and once you begin, you'll find it easier to continue.

   o **Example**: You start washing dishes, and after 5 minutes, you realize it's actually not as hard as you thought, and you continue for another 15 minutes until the kitchen is completely cleaned.

3. **Observe your progress**: After the timer goes off, ask yourself:

   o Did I feel less resistance once I started?

   o Could I continue beyond 5 minutes?

4. **Action**: If you feel ready to keep going, set another 5-minute timer. Keep repeating this until the task is complete or you reach a natural stopping point.

The Right Timing

Goal: To understand the importance of taking action at the right moment and to help you recognize when the time is right.

Instructions:

1. **Think of a past experience** where you took action at the right time.

   - **example**: A person started investing in stocks during a market dip, and it paid off in the long run because they recognized the right time to invest.

   - What was the situation?

   - How did you recognize that it was the right time to act?

   - What were the results of your timely action?

2. **Think of a time when you missed an opportunity** because you didn't take action at

the right time.

- o **Example**: Maybe you had a chance to apply for a job that you were interested in, but you waited until the deadline passed. The job opportunity is now gone.

- o What was the opportunity?

- o Why did you hesitate or delay?

- o How did missing that moment affect you?

3. **Identify patterns**: Look for common themes in both situations.

- o How can you better recognize the right timing for opportunities in your life today?

4. **Action**: Next time an opportunity arises, ask yourself: "Is this the right moment?" Use your past experiences as guidance to take timely action.

Time Blocking for Priorities

Goal: To help you structure your day to ensure that important tasks are prioritized and completed.

Instructions:

1. **List your priorities for the week**: Identify 3-5 key tasks that are most important for achieving your goals.

    example: You want to start a blog, improve your health, and spend quality time with family. These are your top 3 priorities.

2. **Create a time-blocking schedule**: For each day of the week, assign a specific time block to each of your priority tasks.

    o For example, you might block out 9 AM to 11 AM for writing, 12 PM to 1 PM for lunch, and 2 PM to 4 PM for meetings.

- ○ **Example**: If family time is a priority, you might block 6 PM to 8 PM every evening for dinner and activities with family.

3. **Stick to your schedule**: As much as possible, try to stick to your time blocks. If something urgent comes up, adjust your schedule for the day, but try to stay on track for the most important tasks.

4. **Review at the end of the week**: At the end of the week, assess how well you followed your schedule. Were there tasks that got ignored? Were there distractions that slowed you down? Use this feedback to refine your approach for next week.

The Power of Now

Goal: To overcome procrastination by focusing on the present moment and taking immediate action.

Instructions:

1. **Pick one task** you've been procrastinating on. It can be something big or small — the key is that it's something you've been putting off.

   - **example**: You've been putting off organizing your workspace for weeks, even though it's cluttered and distracting you from being productive.

2. **Ask yourself:** "What can I do right now to move forward on this task?"

   - Even if the action is tiny, make a commitment to act immediately.

   - **Example**: You might commit to spending just 5 minutes clearing off your desk, or organizing one small area of your room.

3. **Take immediate action**: Set a timer for 10 minutes and work on the task.

   o Focus on just getting started, not on finishing everything.

   o Even if you stop after 10 minutes, you've taken action, and that's progress.

4. **Reflect**: How did you feel after starting? Did the task seem less overwhelming once you began?

   o **Example**: After just 10 minutes of organizing, you might find the task easier than expected and continue for another 20 minutes

NOTES: *(My learning from this chapter)*

⊙ Now Affirmations Time :

>>   Take a deep breath, feel the energy within you, and read the affirmations out loud with belief <<

- *Every moment is a fresh opportunity.*

- *I am mindful of how I spend my time.*

- *I trust the perfect timing of my actions.*

- *I listen to my inner guidance and move at the right time.*

- *I show up on time and follow through.*

- *I value being present at the right moment.*

6. Not Perfect, Just Consistent

Why Is Consistency Important?

Let me explain this with a real example from my experience as a coach. I meet many people who come to me wanting to learn something new, to change their lives. One such person was a lady named Suvarna.

Suvarna had once learned meditation and even practiced it seriously for about 10 to 12 days. She had experienced how calming and powerful it could be. So now, she didn't just *know* about meditation — she had actually done it. She had tasted the benefits.

But soon, life happened.

Responsibilities piled up. She got caught in the daily grind. And meditation? It quietly slipped out of her routine. When I asked her why she stopped, she said,
 "I just don't have the time. There's too much going on. Meditation takes a back seat."

And yet, she would still tell others how amazing meditation is. She had the knowledge — but not the consistency. And even though she knew how beneficial it was, her life hadn't improved. She was still struggling with health issues, financial stress, and emotional pressure.

That's when she came to me for guidance.

I asked her just one question:
"Suvarna, those 10 days when you practiced meditation — how did you feel?"

She smiled and said,
"Those were the best days. I felt calm, focused, and in control."

So I gently told her,
"Great. Let's start again — but keep it simple. Just do half the time you used to. Even 5 or 10 minutes is enough. But do it every single day. And every day, write down how you felt after the practice."

And then she said something beautiful that stayed with me:
"You're right, Ma'am. I *do* have time — at least for something that's good for me."

So she committed for just 21 days.

And slowly, magic happened.

She started feeling better — calmer, more energetic, clearer in her decisions. Her health began to improve. Her financial situation started to shift. Her mind became more peaceful. She started showing up better in all areas of life. Her consistency gave her clarity, and clarity gave her strength.

And you know the most inspiring part?
Her children saw her change — and they started meditating too.
Suvarna didn't need to *tell* them. She *became* the example. Because when one person transforms, the ripple effect begins at home.

Today, Suvarna's life is stable, strong, and more peaceful than ever — not because she worked harder, but because she showed up with consistency.

That's the power of doing something small — but doing it every day. That's the power of consistency.

How to Maintain Consistency

Consistency is the secret ingredient that turns dreams into reality. It's the daily, unwavering commitment to your goals, even when motivation fades or obstacles appear. Without consistency, the best intentions can remain just that—intentions. In this chapter, we'll explore how to cultivate consistency in your life, no matter the goal.

1. gratitude practice

Before we jump into big actions, let's talk about gratitude. You might think, "What does saying thank you have to do with my goals?"

But here's the truth: when you start your day with gratitude, you shift your energy. You focus on what you *have*, not what you lack. And that keeps you grounded and motivated to keep going.

My friend Rashmi was trying to start a small handmade jewelry business. Every day, she wrote one thing she was thankful for in her business journal—even if it was just, "Today I found a perfect bead." Some days were slow, with no sales at all. But this one-minute gratitude habit reminded her why she started. And guess what? That simple shift in energy helped her stay consistent—her business now ships across the country.

Try This: Write down three things you're grateful for every night. Let this feeling of abundance carry you into the next day.

2. The Power of Small Steps

Big dreams can often feel overwhelming, but they're built step by step. The secret to maintaining consistency is breaking your big goals into small, manageable tasks. It's easier to stay consistent when you only need to focus on one small step at a time.

Example:
Let's say your goal is to get fit. If you think about running a marathon, it might be intimidating. But if you focus on running just 10 minutes a day, you'll be amazed at how consistent you can be. Over time, these small actions compound into big results.

Bonus Tip:
Every day, ask yourself, "What is one small thing I can do today to move closer to my goal?" It's those tiny actions that accumulate into massive progress.

3. Create a Routine That Works for You

Consistency thrives in routine. Establishing a daily or weekly routine sets up a structure that helps you stay on track. But the key is to build a routine that works for your lifestyle—not a rigid one that leaves you feeling burnt out.

Real-Life Example:

I've seen many people start a daily morning workout routine only to give up after a few weeks. Why? They didn't consider their other commitments, like family time or work. When they created a morning routine that allowed flexibility—such as a 20-minute workout instead of an hour—they were more likely to stick with it.

Bonus Tip::

Start by identifying your most productive times of the day. Design your routine around those periods. Whether it's the morning, afternoon, or evening, consistency grows when you work with your natural energy.

4. Celebrate Small Wins

Consistency can sometimes feel monotonous. That's why celebrating small wins is so important.

Recognizing the little milestones not only reinforces your actions but also keeps you motivated for the next step.

Example:
Imagine you're trying to save money. Rather than waiting until you've reached your savings goal to celebrate, why not celebrate each milestone? You could reward yourself when you save your first ₹1,000, ₹5,000, and so on. This helps maintain motivation and makes the process feel less like a chore.

Bonus Tip:
Set achievable mini-goals and celebrate them. You don't need to wait for the big finish line to give yourself credit.

5. Build Accountability into Your Process

One of the strongest drivers of consistency is accountability. When we know someone else is depending on us, we're far more likely to follow through.

Example:

I once helped a friend start a reading habit. We decided that every week, we'd share what we had read with each other. Having that external accountability kept her on track, and she ended up reading 12 books in a year.

Bonus Tip:

Find a friend, mentor, or group that you can check in with regularly. Accountability doesn't have to be formal—it can simply be a weekly check-in where you share your progress and challenges.

6. Manage Setbacks with Patience

No one is perfect, and setbacks are a part of the journey. The key to consistency isn't perfection; it's resilience. When things don't go according to plan, be kind to yourself and keep going.

Example:

I know someone who wanted to lose weight and had a solid plan. However, they faced setbacks like missed workouts and bad food choices. Instead of quitting, they focused on getting back to their routine the next day. They realized that setbacks weren't failures but simply part of the process.

Bonus Tip:

If you miss a day or face a challenge, don't let guilt or frustration derail your efforts. Acknowledge the setback, learn from it, and get back on track. Progress is about persistence, not perfection.

7. Visualize Your Success

Visualization is a powerful tool for maintaining consistency. When you imagine your success vividly, you create a mental connection that drives you to continue. It's not just about seeing the end goal; it's about feeling the emotions tied to your success.

Example:

Before starting my weight loss journey, I would picture myself feeling strong, confident, and healthy. This mental image kept me focused, especially on tough days when motivation was low.

Bonus Tip:

Take a few minutes each day to close your eyes and visualize what achieving your goal will look like and feel like. Feel the pride, joy, and relief of reaching that milestone.

8. Reflect Regularly

Maintaining consistency isn't a one-time thing; it's an ongoing process. Regularly reflecting on your progress helps you stay connected to your "why" and gives you the chance to adjust if needed.

Example:

I have a weekly habit of journaling my progress toward my goals. This helps me understand what's working, what needs improvement, and keeps me motivated to keep going. It's also a great way to recognize how far I've come.

Bonus Tip:

Take time at the end of each week to review your progress. Reflect on what went well, what didn't, and how you can adjust your approach in the coming days.

⊙ *Now implementation time*

1. Clarity Check

- **Objective**: Understand what your goal is, and ensure you have a clear vision of what you want to achieve.

- **Exercise**:

  - Write down one goal you want to achieve. Be specific. For example: "I want to exercise for 20 minutes every day."

  - Ask yourself:

    - Is this goal clear and specific enough?

    - Do I know exactly what actions are needed to achieve this goal?

2. Create Your Daily Routine

- **Objective**: Build a routine that supports your goal and sets you up for consistency.

- **Exercise**:

  - Identify a time of day when you are most energetic. Write down your ideal routine for that time, which includes your goal.

- Example: "I will exercise every morning for 20 minutes after breakfast."

- Does your routine fit seamlessly into your day? Can you stick to it for at least a week?

3. Identify Obstacles

- **Objective**: Recognize any challenges that might stop you from staying consistent.

- **Exercise**:

  - List 3 potential obstacles that could prevent you from being consistent with your goal (e.g., lack of time, distractions, low motivation).

  - Next, write down solutions for each obstacle.

- Example: "If I'm too tired, I can try a 10-minute workout instead of 20 minutes to stay on track."

4. Small Wins Tracker

- **Objective**: Celebrate small wins to build momentum.

- **Exercise**:

  - Write down 5 small steps you can take towards your goal this week. These should be actions that are easy to complete and fit into your day.

  - Example: "Today, I will walk for 10 minutes."

  - At the end of the week, reflect on the small wins. How did these actions help you stay consistent?

5. Accountability Partner

- **Objective**: Create an external source of support to stay accountable.

- **Exercise**:

  - Find a friend, family member, or colleague who can help keep you accountable for your goal.

  - Write down their name and how you will check in with them (e.g., a weekly call, text, or meeting).

  - Ask them to check in with you once a week and share your progress.

6. Reflection on Setbacks

- **Objective**: Learn from setbacks and continue moving forward.

- **Exercise**:

  - Write down any setbacks you've experienced while trying to maintain consistency in the past.

- o What were the main reasons for these setbacks? (E.g., lack of motivation, distractions, life events)

- o What can you do differently next time?

- o How can you stay resilient and continue your goal despite these challenges?

7. Visualize Success

- **Objective**: Use visualization to stay motivated.

- **Exercise**:

  - o Take a few moments to sit quietly and close your eyes. Imagine yourself achieving your goal.

  - o Visualize how it feels, what you see, and who is around you. Write down this experience in detail.

- How does this visualization inspire you to take the first step today?

8. Weekly Reflection

- **Objective**: Reflect on your progress and adjust your plan as needed.

- **Exercise**:

  - At the end of the week, reflect on your progress towards your goal.

  - Ask yourself:

    - Did I stick to my plan consistently?

    - What worked well this week? What didn't?

    - What adjustments can I make for next week to stay on track?

Bonus Tip: Consistency Affirmation

- Write down an affirmation that motivates you
  to stay consistent. Repeat it to yourself every
  morning or before you take action.

Example: "I am committed to my goals, and I take
small, consistent steps every

NOTES: *(My learning this chapter)*

⊙ Now Affirmations Time :

>>   Take a deep breath, feel the energy within you, and read the affirmations out loud with belief <<

<u>Affirmations for Maintaining Consistency</u>

- *"I am committed to my goals, and I take consistent action every day."*

- *"Each small step I take leads me closer to my desired outcome."*

- *"I embrace my journey and stay consistent, even when challenges arise."*

- *"Consistency is the key to my success, and I trust in my ability to stay on course."*

- *"I am strong enough to continue moving forward, even on tough days."*

- *"My dedication to my goals is unwavering, and I keep pushing forward, no matter what."*

- *"I celebrate each small victory, as it brings me closer to my big goal."*

- *"I create routines that support my success and make consistency feel easy and natural."*

- *"With every small action, I am building a future of success and fulfillment."*

7. Change Is a Choice, Made Real by Action

Change doesn't happen by chance.
It begins with a **clear decision** — and becomes real when we **take action**.

> You don't need to be perfect.
> You just need to **begin**.

Every small step you take is a sign that you're choosing growth, strength, and a better life.

Knowing is not enough. Doing is what makes the difference.

> *"Your life will not change just because you want it to. It will change when you act on it."*

Change is not something that happens *to* us; it's something we choose to create.
The power to transform lies in the **choices** we make

— and the **actions** we take to bring those choices to life.

It all begins with a decision.
You must decide what you want, and then **commit to taking the necessary actions** to make it real. Every moment is an opportunity to implement the change you desire.

Action, no matter how small, is what moves you forward.
The road may not always be easy, but each step, no matter how small, is a part of your journey toward the life you want.

> *"Your future is shaped by the actions you take today. The choice is yours. The action is yours. The change is yours."*

⊙ *Now implementation time*

Choose Your Change

Step 1:

Think of one area in your life where you truly want to see a change.

(Example: Health, Career, Relationships, Finances, Personal Growth.)

Step 2:

Answer these reflection questions:

1. ***What change do I want to make?***
   → *(Be very clear.)*

2. ***Why do I want this change?***
   → *(Write your deep reason.)*

3. ***What first action can I take today?***
   → *(Small action, even tiny is fine.)*

4. ***What will happen if I don't take action?***
   ➜ *(Think honestly.)*

5. ***My Commitment Statement:***
   ➜ *"I choose to change by taking action now because _______."*

Example:

1. ***Change I Want:*** *Improve my fitness.*

2. ***Why:*** *To feel energetic and confident.*

3. ***First Action:*** *Go for a 15-minute walk today evening.*

4. ***If I Don't Act:*** *I will feel tired and regret missing another day.*

5. ***Commitment Statement:***
   ➜ *"I choose to change by taking action now because my health is my true wealth."*

NOTES: *(My learning from this chapter)*

⊙ Now Affirmations Time :

>>   Take a deep breath, feel the energy within you, and read the affirmations out loud with belief <<

- *I am the creator of my own change.*

- *I choose growth, and I take action to make it real.*

- *Every small step I take brings me closer to the life I desire.*

- *I trust that my actions will create the life I've always dreamed of.*

- *I am empowered to turn my choices into results.*

- *My future is shaped by the actions I take today.*

- *I don't wait for the perfect moment. I create the moment through action.*

- *I am capable of making real change through focused action.*

- *Change is a choice I make every day with courage and confidence.*

- *I am committed to the journey of transformation and progress.*

- *— I embrace change as a natural part of my growth.*

- *My actions today are creating the life I want tomorrow.*

- *I trust myself to make choices that lead to positive change.*

- *Each day, I am taking steps toward the person I want to become.*

- *I am capable of turning my dreams into reality through action.*

- *I release fear and step into action with confidence.*

- *I choose to take action, no matter how small, to create progress.*

- *The more I act, the more my life transforms.*

- *I am the architect of my future through the actions I take now.*

- *I am in charge of my life and the choices I make create lasting change.*

8. Power of "NO" and "YES" in Implementations

1. Power of "NO"

When we begin a transformation journey, especially in any area of life, two words become very important: *YES* and *NO*.

Let me share my own example.

When I started my weight loss journey, I made a simple but strong rule for myself:
"No eating after 7 PM."

This was not a diet plan someone gave me. It was my own decision — a personal promise I made to myself with love and discipline.

In the beginning, it wasn't easy. Many times, friends or relatives invited me to their homes for dinner.

They'd lovingly say:

"Come on, it's just one day — have a little, what's the big deal?"

But here's what I realized — it's never *just one day.*

Today it's one friend's invitation,
15 days later, it's someone else,
And slowly, it continues.

If we keep breaking our rules for every small occasion, when will we ever choose what's truly good for us?

I didn't want to hurt anyone's feelings, but I also had to ask myself —

"How much do I respect my own promises?"
"When will I do what is right for *me*?"

So I stayed firm and replied gently:

"Please understand, I really don't eat after 7 PM."

Yes, it felt uncomfortable in the beginning.
Sometimes awkward.

Sometimes guilty.
But I kept going. I kept honoring my word.

And do you know what happened?

Now, everyone — my family, my friends, my community — they all know:

"Varsha won't eat after 7 PM."

I no longer have to explain myself. People have started respecting my boundaries.

That is the power of **saying NO with love**.
It protects your progress.
It trains the world around you to support your goals.
And most importantly —
It builds your inner strength.

Because when you say **NO** to the things that take you away from your goals,
You are actually saying **YES** to your dreams.

>> Let me share one more recent example of a client who came to me, a 17-year-old boy named *Rohit*.

He was a smart student, a rank holder, and came from a good family. But he reached out to me because he was struggling with something he couldn't share with his parents.

Rohit had a close group of friends — all of them were top students in class. One day, during an outing, one of them casually said,
 "Let's try beer today, just for fun."
 Some boys hesitated and said, *"No, this isn't right."*
Even Rohit said the same.
 But out of the five, three agreed.

And when the majority said "yes," Rohit didn't want to be the odd one out.
 So they bought a single bottle and shared it among the five of them.
 They didn't get caught. Nothing seemed wrong.
It felt like a "safe thrill."

Two months passed. They did it again. Then again.
 Before they knew it, it became a monthly habit.
 Not much — just enough that no one at home would notice.
But it was still there. Still wrong.

A whole year passed like this.

But deep down, Rohit started feeling uncomfortable.
 He felt guilty — especially around his parents.
 He knew this wasn't the path he wanted to walk on.
 But every time he tried to say *no* to his friends, the fear stopped him.

"What if they stop talking to me?"
 "What if I'm left alone?"
 "What if I lose all my friends?"

That's when he came to me.

He looked me in the eye and said,
 "Ma'am, I don't want this in my life anymore. I want to quit."

I asked him one simple question:
 "Rohit, do you truly believe drinking beer is wrong for you?"
 He said, **"Yes, ma'am. I know it's wrong."**

Then I asked,
 "So why can't you say no to your friends?"

He replied,
 "Because I feel if I say no, they might leave me. I'll be alone. I'll lose them."

So I asked him again:
 "Do your friends know it's wrong?"
He said, **"Yes, they know."**

I asked,
 "Then do real friends ever force someone into doing something wrong?"
"No," he said softly.

I smiled and said,
 "Then they're not friends, Rohit. They're just people who want company for fun — not for your good."

That hit him.

I told him,
 "Every time they ask you to drink, just remember — they're not thinking about you. They're thinking about themselves. If you truly care about your future, it's time to choose yourself. Say no, not to them, but to the situation that's not serving you."

From that point on, Rohit slowly started saying "no."
 Not just with words — but with strength.
 He stopped being afraid of losing people.
 Instead, he found the courage to choose what's right for himself.

Today, he has completely stopped drinking.
And the truth is — he didn't lose all his friends.
He only lost the ones who were not true friends in the first place.

Now, whenever something doesn't feel right,
he calmly says,
"No. This is not for me."

That's the real power of saying "No."

2. Power of "YES"

Saying **"YES"** means **opening the door to opportunities, growth, and action**.

It is the first step towards real change.
When you say **YES** to yourself and your goals, you start moving forward with confidence.

One of my students named **Bharti** who always dreamed of being fit and healthy.
Every day, she would tell herself,

"Tomorrow I will start exercising,"

but tomorrow never came.

She kept waiting... until one morning, she looked at herself in the mirror and said loudly:
"YES, I will start today!"

That single **YES** changed everything.

Shree didn't start with big plans.

She simply put on her shoes and walked for 5 minutes.

The next day, she said **YES** again — 5 minutes became 10 minutes.

The next day, she said **YES** again — 10 minutes became 20 minutes.

She decided to do it for just 21 days.

Slowly, her body and mind got used to walking every day.

Step by step, her body and mind started becoming balanced.

Slowly, her body became stronger, her mind became sharper, and her confidence grew.

⊙ *Now implementation time*

Saying "YES" and "NO" for Your Goals

Step 1: Identify Your Goal

Write one important goal you are working toward:

Step 2: List Things You Must Say "YES" To

Write down the positive actions or habits you must accept:

> Example:

- YES to daily 30 minutes of exercise

- YES to healthy eating

- YES to focused study time

Now your list:
>

Step 3: List Things You Must Say "NO" To
Write the distractions or bad habits you must avoid:
> Example:

- NO to late-night junk food

- NO to mindless scrolling on phone

- NO to negative thinking

Now your list:

>

Step 4: Make Your Personal Power Statement

Complete this sentence:

> "I choose to say YES to _________ and NO to _________ because I respect my dreams."

____

____

____

$ **Goal:** Lose 5 kg weight.

YES To:

 * Eat my food with respect

* I enjoyed my food

 * 7 hours of good sleep
 * Morning walk

* dinner before 7 pm

NO To:

dinner after 7pm

Eating in a hurry,

watching TV or using the mobile while eating.

Sugar
 cold drink

Power Statement:

"I choose to say YES to my health and NO to unhealthy habits because I respect my body and my life."

NOTES: *(My learning from this chapter)*

⊙ Now Affirmations Time :

>>   Take a deep breath, feel the energy within you, and read the affirmations out loud with belief <<

- *"I say NO to distractions that pull me away from my goals."*

- *"I lovingly say NO to anything that doesn't serve my growth."*

- *"My NO protects my dreams and my energy."*

- *"Every NO I say is a YES to my bigger purpose."*

- *"I feel strong and clear when I say NO to what is not right for me."*

- *"I say YES to opportunities that align with my dreams."*

- *"I say YES to consistent action every day."*

- *"My YES opens the door to success and new beginnings."*

- *"I trust my YES to guide me towards my best life."*

- *"I say YES to growth, courage, and transformation."*
- *"I say NO to fear and YES to faith."*
- *"I say NO to excuses and YES to action."*

- *"I say NO to doubt and YES to my dreams."*

- *"I say NO to old habits and YES to new possibilities."*

- *"I say NO to delays and YES to now!"*

9. Case Studies & Success Stories

My journey as *Author*

Writing *"You Can Change Your Life By Law of Implementation"* wasn't just about sharing ideas—it became my own biggest lesson in implementation. I went through the same things many of us do: doubts, distractions, life pulling me in all directions. But I stayed with it. And this is how it all unfolded.

The Dream

Like so many people, I had a dream. I always wanted to write a book.
I had so many thoughts, so much to say.
I'd imagine the cover, the title, the impact.

But you know what? Dreaming alone wasn't enough.

I had to *do something*.

The real shift happened when I told myself,

"Okay, Varsha—it's time to stop dreaming and start doing."

The Procrastination Phase

Let's be honest — this part was real.

I'd open my laptop, start writing… then stop halfway to scroll, make tea, fold laundry.
Sometimes, I was just scared:
"What if it's not good?" "What if no one reads it?"

But deep inside, I knew this truth: *Nothing moves until you do.*

So, I decided to take small, consistent actions.

Not chapters in a day—just paragraphs. Sometimes just bullet points.

But I did it every day. That's how the fog started to clear.

>> *Implementation in Action*

Once I truly committed, I treated this book like a promise.
 I set mini-goals:

 "Write one section." "Edit 500 words." "Just open the draft and touch it today."

Even on tough days—when I was tired, cranky, or questioning everything—I'd do something.
 Not perfectly. But consistently.
 And that made all the difference.

The Power of Saying "No"

This was hard. Saying no to random chai plans, late-night scrolling, and even some fun events.
 Not because I didn't care, but because *I cared deeply*—about this dream.

Slowly, people around me started noticing.
 They respected the boundary. They saw I meant business.

And "No" stopped feeling rude—it started feeling powerful.

The Breakthrough

Then one day… I looked at my manuscript and realized—
"It's done."

Not perfect. Not final. But it was real.
My heart was in those pages. My lessons, my stories, my voice.

And that moment? That's when I truly understood the power of implementation.

Before Implementation: The Old Me

Let me take you back a bit.
Before all this began, I was the girl with a head full of ideas… but no action.

I'd say, "I want to write a book someday."
Then I'd doubt myself:
"Who will read it?"

"Is it even worth writing?"
"Maybe I'm not good enough?"

I was stuck in the dream zone.

Turning Point

One ordinary day, something clicked:
> *A dream stays a dream until you act on it.*

So, I started small.

 A few lines. A rough outline. A quiet promise to myself.
 I told myself:
 "You don't have to be perfect. You just have to keep showing up."

And that changed everything.

If you're holding on to a dream, wondering if it's possible—let me tell you: it is.
 You don't need a perfect plan. You need a starting point.
 And the courage to keep going, one small step at a time.

Richa's Jewelry Journey: From Hobby to Business

Richa always loved making jewelry. Her dream? To sell it across India. But with a full-time job and house responsibilities, consistency felt hard.

So, she did one thing daily: work 20 minutes on her jewelry, no matter what. Some days she just cleaned beads. Other days she created one design. And every single night, she wrote one thing she was grateful for in her business journal.

After 6 months, she had 30+ designs, an Instagram page, and her first 10 customers. Within a year, she was shipping to five different states!

What worked? Tiny daily action + gratitude. Not magic. Just momentum.

Vikram's Fitness Fix: 5 Minutes to 5K

Vikram was the "I'll start Monday" type. Every Sunday night, he'd plan workouts. By Wednesday, he'd quit.

One day, he told himself, "Just 5 minutes of walking. That's it." And he did. Day after day. Some days were just 5 minutes. Other days, he'd walk 30 without realizing.

Three months later? He ran his first 5K.

What worked? He dropped the 'all or nothing' mindset and chose consistency over intensity.

Neha's Savings Celebration: Small Wins, Big Smile

Neha wanted to save ₹1,00,000. But the number felt scary.

So, she broke it into ₹500 chunks. Every time she saved ₹500, she coloured a square on her wall chart and treated herself to something fun (like a fancy coffee or a new pen).

Not only did she hit her goal early, but she *enjoyed* saving for the first time in her life.

What worked? Making the journey playful and visual. Motivation stayed high because the process felt rewarding.

Rahul's Reading Habit: Buddy Power!

Rahul wanted to read more but always scrolled Instagram instead. One day, his friend challenged him: "Let's read one chapter a day. We'll talk every Friday."

That buddy system worked wonders. Knowing someone would ask, "So, what did you read?" kept him accountable.

By the end of the year, Rahul had finished 14 books.

What worked? A reading buddy who cared and weekly check-ins that made quitting harder.

Priya's Comeback Story: Bouncing Back with Grace

Priya was on a healthy eating journey. Things were going great—until wedding season hit. Sweets, late nights, skipped meals.

She felt disappointed, but then remembered something she read: "A bad day is just that. A *day*."

She didn't throw the whole plan away. She simply got back to her routine the next morning. And because she didn't let guilt win, she stayed on track in the long run.

What worked? Kindness toward herself and quick recovery after setbacks.

These stories are proof: You don't need to be perfect. You just need to be consistent in your *own way*. Whether it's 5 minutes a day, tiny savings, or reading with a buddy—what matters most is that you keep showing up.

Let these people be your reminder: If they can do it, so can you.

1. My life after Implementations

After – Becoming the Author

- Today, I have written my book:
  "You Can Change Your Life by Law of Implementation."

- I feel confident, clear, and proud.

- I turned my idea into something real.

- Now I want to help others do the same — take action and see results.

"Before, I only dreamed. Now, I take action."

10. Tools to Implementation

1. Weekly Action Planner

Purpose: To help my readers break your goals into small, trackable steps over 7 days.

Write Goal of the Week:

____

____

Why it matters:

____

____

Top 3 Actions This Week:

1. ______________________________

2. ______________________________

3. ______________________________

Weekly Schedule:

Mon: ______________________________

Tue: ______________________________

Wed: ______________________________

Thu: ______________________________

Fri: ______________________________

Sat: ______________________________

Sun: ______________________________

Reflection:

\# What did I complete?

\# What needs to continue?

\# What did I learn this week?

2. Implementation Tracker

Purpose: To track consistency, mindset, and progress toward implementation.

Implementation Area: ______________________________

Start Date: ____________

End Date: ____________

Day	Task Completed	Felt Focused?	Notes
Mon	yes /no	yes /no	
Tue	yes /no	yes /no	
wed	yes /no	yes /no	
Thu	yes /no	yes /no	
Fri	yes /no	yes /no	
Sat	yes /no	yes /no	
sun	yes /no	yes /no	

Weekly Progress Summary:

____

____

____

____

____

Here are some more *Bonus tools or worksheets* that can be valuable additions to your book, enhancing your reader's journey in implementing the concepts discussed in each chapter:

1. Daily Action Tracker

- **Purpose:** To track your daily implementation progress.

- **How to Use:**

  - **Every day, note down one small action you took toward your goal.**

  - **Reflect on how it felt and any challenges you faced.**

  - **Over time, you'll see how consistent effort adds up.**

Example of Action Tracker Table:

TABLE

Date	Action Taken	Thoughts/Challenges	Emotion/Feeling
dd/mm/yyyy	Wrote 500 words for my book	Felt a little unsure but pushed through	Proud of the progress made
dd/mm/yyyy	Meditated for 10 minutes	Struggled with distractions	Felt calm and focused

2. Weekly Implementation Planner

- **Purpose:** To create a detailed plan for implementing tasks over the course of a week.

- **How to Use:**

  - Write down the main goal you're focusing on for the week.

  - Break it down into smaller tasks and assign a day to each task.

  - At the end of the week, review your progress and tweak your approach if needed.

- **Example of Weekly Planner Table:**

Goal for the Week:

Day

Monday

Tuesday

Wednesday

Thursday

Friday

---

3. Goal Reflection Sheet

- **Purpose: To reflect on your goals and progress regularly.**

- **How to Use:**

    - **Reflect on the goals you've set, whether they are long-term or short-term.**

    - **Ask yourself the following questions:**

        - **How close am I to achieving this goal?**

        - **What obstacles have I faced and how did I overcome them?**

        - **What adjustments do I need to make?**

○ **Use this sheet to re-align yourself when you feel stuck or unsure.**

● **Example of Goal Reflection Sheet:**

Goal:

____

–

Current Status:

____

What's Working Well:

____

What Needs Improvement:

____

Action Steps to Move Forward:

____

4. Mindset Shifts Worksheet

- **Purpose: To help readers identify and overcome limiting beliefs that hinder implementation.**

- **How to Use:**

  - **Ask yourself what negative beliefs or self-talk have been stopping you from taking action.**

  - **Write down each belief, and then challenge it with a more empowering belief.**

  - **Focus on shifting your mindset as you work towards your goals.**

- **Example of Mindset Shifts Worksheet:**

Limiting Belief

1. "I'm not good enough to succeed."

Empowering Belief

1. "I have the ability to succeed, I just need to keep trying."

2. **"I can find time for what matters if I prioritize."**

5. Progress and Gratitude Journal

- **Purpose:** To reflect on your achievements and express gratitude as part of the process.

- **How to Use:**

    - At the end of each day or week, write down:

        - 1 thing you're grateful for that day.

        - 1 thing you've accomplished toward your goal.

        - 1 thing you want to improve on.

    - This journal will keep you motivated by highlighting your progress and maintaining a positive mindset.

Example of Progress and Gratitude Journal:

Date: _________________________

Gratitude: I am grateful for my support system.

Progress: Completed writing the first draft of Chapter 3.

Improvements Needed: Need to manage time better to avoid procrastination.

6. Visualization Worksheet

- **Purpose: To visualize the success you are working toward.**

- **How to Use:**

  - **Close your eyes and take a few deep breaths.**

  - **Picture yourself achieving your goal and what that would feel like.**

  - **Write down the details: What do you see? What do you feel? How do you celebrate your success?**

- **Example of Visualization Worksheet:**

Visualization: "I imagine myself speaking confidently at my book launch event."

What I see: A room full of people, a microphone in hand, and smiles everywhere.

What I feel: Proud, joyful, and grateful.

How I celebrate: Thank my readers and team for their support.

7. Action Habit Tracker

- **Purpose:** To build daily habits that support your goal and help you implement consistently.

- **How to Use:**

    - **Choose a habit that supports your goal (e.g., reading 10 pages of a book every day, walking 20 minutes, or practicing gratitude).**

    - **Track it every day to stay consistent and motivated.**

- **Example of Habit Tracker Table:**

Habit:

____

____

____

NOTES: *(My learning from this chapter)*

Conclusion

As I look back now, I feel a deep sense of gratitude and pride. Writing this book has been a beautiful journey for me, and it's not just a book; it's a reflection of my own growth, my struggles, and my Milestones

When I first began, I knew I had something important to share. I wanted to help others understand that real change doesn't happen all at once. It's not about sudden, big steps—it's about the small, everyday actions we take. This book is my way of showing you that change is possible through consistent effort. I've experienced this firsthand, and I believe that you can experience the same transformation in your life.

As I wrote, I learned more about myself. The more I shared my thoughts with you, the more I realized how powerful the Law of Implementation really is. It's not just a set of steps—it's a way of living. It's about taking what we know, what we've learned, and putting it into action. Every little step you take toward your goals is progress. That's the truth I've learned through my own journey.

I want you to know that no matter where you are in life right now, change is possible. It doesn't matter what area of life you want to improve—whether it's your health, your job, your relationships, or your personal growth. The key to making it happen is simple: take action. You don't have to wait for the "perfect" time, because the perfect time is always now. Start with small steps. Be patient with yourself. And most importantly, trust the process.

This book isn't just for you—it's been a guide for me too. Writing it has reminded me of the power of taking consistent action. It has shown me that no matter how tough things get, we can always move forward, step by step. Change isn't easy, but it's always worth it.

I hope that through reading this book, you have found the encouragement and strength to take the first step toward your own goals. Remember, you don't have to be perfect to begin. You just have to begin. And with every step you take, you're getting closer to where you want to be.

Thank you for being a part of this journey with me. I believe in you. I believe in your ability to make the changes you want in your life. Keep going, keep believing in yourself, and keep taking action. You are on the right path. The best is yet to come.

With all my heart,

Varsha

⦿ Affirmations Time :

- *I believe in my ability to create meaningful change in my life.*

- *Every step I take brings me closer to my goals and dreams.*

- *I am proud of how far I've come, and I'm excited for where I'm going.*

- *Change is possible for me, and I am open to every opportunity it brings.*

- *I trust the process of growth, knowing that small steps lead to big results.*

- *I am worthy of the transformation I seek in my life.*

- *With every challenge, I grow stronger and more resilient.*

- *I am committed to taking consistent action every day toward my goals.*

- *My journey is unique, and I embrace the path I am walking.*

- *I am ready for the best chapters of my life to unfold.*

- *I have the power to turn my dreams into reality, one step at a time.*

- *I celebrate my progress, and I honor my growth every day.*

- *I trust myself to make decisions that align with my purpose and values.*

- *I am the author of my own story, and I write the next chapter with courage and faith.*

- *Every challenge is an opportunity for me to grow, learn, and become stronger.*

Some Important Reviews:

Vishwashree sonaskar

My thoughts about the book "You Can Change Your Life Through Law of Implementation". This law help me a lot in my life to everywhere till date . The idea of this book is amazing. That how it can change many peoples life and make their life easier and guide them give them a path towards there goals. One example that i have implemented is that I thought that I should achieve 30 above marks in all subjects out of 40 and it happened exactly as i thought so I implemented in my life. This law of implementation should be there in everyones life to make their life easier and everyone ahoyld know about it . But this thing only works if you have trust and the examples which are there in the book are real. The practises which are given in the book will also help you a lot to be consistent. This are my thoughts about the book. It is a great book. Wonderful work done by my mom.

Connect with me on:

Instagram:

Facebook:

9 7 9 8 8 8 9 9 6 1 4 3 4 7